TO

JAMES

Bill Sessoms

MISTER BILL

THE POWER
of LOVE

Inspirations
Poems
Prose
Ponderings

MISTER BILL

PAGE PUBLISHING, INC.
New York, NY

First originally published by Page Publishing, Inc. 2019

ISBN 978-1-68456-629-7 (Hardcover)
ISBN 978-1-68456-630-3 (Digital)

Printed in the United States of America

It's all up to you to make it right,
Jesus will guide you.

CONTENTS

Inspirations

Poems

Prose

Pondering

INSPIRATIONS

LEADS ME HOME

The day he leads me home, I'll be so happy at his throne.
I'll stand before him then, no sins to atone.

He smiles at me, so I bow my head. his hand touches my face, and I
become like him.
Music filled with rhapsody of love, with words more beautiful than
my favorite hymn.
His angels come and bring a chair, "This is for you because you care.
It's a place of honor which you have earned."

I look to him, and he says…

"Yes, you have earned your place to live with me.
By faith alone you found your way.
So an angel you will be for all eternity.
I kept an eye on you as you took the steps of life.

I gave you hunger, hardships, and pain.
I broke you down to build you up again.
The test you passed in every way.
You turned away, but then came back.

Your faith grew stronger each time you would turn.
I knew you didn't want to bum.
The choice was yours, as with every man.
I'm glad you chose the Heavenly Band.

I gave you pain to give you wisdom.
I gave you love so you may too.
When you shed a tear, I shed one too.
When you gave a smile, you were smiling for me.

When you said, 'Lord, lead me home,' you showed the faith of a thousand men.

Your work was hard, I made it so.
You loved through it and proud you were when you laid your head down.
I heard your whisper, 'Thank you for the day. Please lead me home.'
You never asked for anything. Somehow you knew I had your hand.

I led you home as you asked. I sent my angels to bring you here.
I knew you loved me from your heart.
When you said, 'Lord, lead me home,'
I knew you wanted to be with me.

When a person prays, 'Lord, lead me home,'
It means I love you, I trust you.
You have shown me your faith that you have a Master that loves you."

CHARITY

I was resting in my swing,
With a smile on my face, feeling like a king.
Smug I was, thinking only of me.
I wish others could be like this.

A knock at the garden gate
Came in the evening late.
A shaggy man stood just outside.
"What do you want?" I asked with a stare.

"A piece of bread, kind sir," he said in a humble tone.
"You see I have no home and I'm cold to the bone.
My job is gone and my wife has died.
My heart is broken and will not mend."

"Why come to me with that sad tale?
I have no use for one like you, no matter how loud you wail.
What I have is mine and I plan to keep it."
I threw a fit until he walked away.

I strolled back to my swing,
And once again began to feel like a king.
I heard a voice speak just within my head,
"That could have been you asking for bread."

My heart sank as I jumped from the swing.
Out of the gate I went with a fling.
"Sir! Sir! Where are you?" I called so loud.
I had to find him to give him some bread.

I sat down, and for what I had done, I cried.
"Sir, do you need some help?" someone said by my side.
There he stood, all shaggy and wet, offering me his help.
I gave him a hug and said, "Come with me."

As I led him back to the garden, not meant just for me.
I said, "This is the place where I want you to be."
I gave him bread and wine,
And I realized we are all of one kind.

My heart sang with a joyous tone,
Because I had helped one man who had been cold to the bone.
What we have, we have because of God's grace.
We must share, for as we give a portion, we get a portion.

Charity…don't be without it!

CONTROL

There is a trait that humans have.
Make no mistake it is in us all.
We try to use it with all our might,
Until we find it is really no use at all.

We love to tell others what to do.
For we think, I know what is best for you.

We even say, "Perk your ears for you must learn from me.
My way is best. I know it all.
But you just know part.
Without my knowledge you will surely fall."

I have had to listen to your brays and thoughts.
But you are not me. I am someone else, not you.

I will find my own way, though I would like your help.
Just please don't tell me what to do.
You cannot control the way I think.
And you should never tell me what to say.

For I have a mind that is all my own
And to me, not to you, it belongs.
You may guide me with your kindness, loving touch, and smiling face.
But don't control me with harsh words, demands, and judging looks.

Your words of wisdom?
They fall flat on my mind that you try to impact.
Control you want, but you can't have.
You have no power over me.

I will listen to what you have to offer,
If you ask with a voice speaking from your heart.
If you don't, then from you, I must depart.
For I must listen to my own heart.

The power you think you have when you try to control,
Is just a myth within your soul.

Control…it destroys!

CRITICISM

Have you ever wondered why someone is critical of you?
Could it be your looks, size, actions, or words have a deficiency?
Or could it be you just don't meet their opinion of what they think
you should be?

It seems that some people think they know best.
And they want you to listen to their every cruel word,
As they smile and say it is for your own good.

But why would another know what is best for you?
Could it be they think they are more important or smarter?
Or maybe they think to heaven they live a little closer.

You are God's child.
If you do wrong, let God tell you so.

Do not criticize another when it is just to satisfy your mind.
Everyone has their own opinion,
And everyone must create their own dominion.

Criticize we must, from time to time.
But when we do, we must make sure our words are building blocks,
And not words used to put down and hurt, like throwing rocks.

Don't let your feelings spill out on someone else.
When you feel like criticizing another human being,
Remember to look at them as God does. Through eyes of love he's
seeing.

Criticism…it's not your best!

FAMILY

The chain that binds a family can never be broken.
The seed has been sown and we are each a token.
Pain and suffering will only make us grow.
If we endure the pain we will surely glow.
Forgiveness is the key.
It makes us what we are meant to be.
All of us need it so we can move on,
To the place where we belong.

FORGIVE

Your deed went awry and put a tear in my eye.
You meant well, but your ire put you in a spell.
Harsh I was when I struck back.
Now there is another with a tear in the eye.

I walked away and all day my heart was sad.
My mood was sullen and full of sorrow.
I wished I could forget the deed was done,
But it would not change.

I felt so bad, but I knew I was right.
And if I was right, she should have a tear in her eye.
My thoughts did not help, so I decided to have a glass.
I needed a belt to try to forget. It didn't help. I had another.

When I got home there was a tear in my eye.
The day had been wasted since I had said my morning bye.
Oh, how I wish I had not struck back,
And in my hurt, giving hurt back.

I looked at her face with no tear in her eye.
I heard her words, "I'm glad you're home.
I've been sad all day long,
Just waiting for you to come back where you belong."

She said, "I am sorry I spoke out of turn.
Will you forgive me for what I did?
My day was wasted, my heart was sad.
So I sat alone and watched the door."

I dropped to my knees and said,
"Oh, it was not you, it was me.
Will you forgive my morning tone?"
I held her tight as I said, "Please forgive me."

"Yes, I will," came a golden tone.
My heart smiled and my eyes cried.
Our tears mixed and fell to the floor.
Forgiveness shows a great form of love.
It is God's love flowing down from above.

Forgive...it will save the day!

GOOD

What good will I be to this day I see?
It is up to me to find the key,
That opens the door for the good in this day.

Who will need me to be my best?
Someone is waiting; I feel it in my chest.
I want to do good; I don't want to hurt.

I'll walk through this day and look for the good.
And if I encounter a bad mood,
I'll try to turn it around into good.

If someone needs a lift,
I'll give them my hand like a gift.
Finding good is not easy; sometimes we need help to see.

I found lots of ways to do good this day.
I just looked for it in the work and the play.
Good is always there; it is everywhere.

Keep your feet on the ground and look from the heart.
You will always be able to do your part.
And you will never be alone when you do good.

For I am there with you, extending my hand too.
Never grow tired of doing good, instead stay true.
How would you feel if I tired of doing good for you?

Be good in all and to all people and things.
You will then see what joy good brings.

Good…it makes you.

HATE

Today I think I want to hate.
For life has made me want to cry.
I cannot think of any reason why,
I should not hate.

My body is old. My mind is going.
There is so much for me to hate.
Why should anyone suffer this fate?
So I'll choose to hate.

I look around and say, "I hate this place."
I look in the mirror and say, "I hate this face."
I step away and say, "Why is this my fate?"
No answer comes. It is getting late and I hate to wait.

So off I go to share my hate.
I have so much of it to give away.
Others will hear me and ask me to stay.
I'll teach them how easy it is to hate.

I tried to form a club for hateful people.
I walked around as their leader, standing tall.
But it seemed no one liked me—not one at all.
They didn't like my words of hate.

It seemed the harder I tried, the less they listened.
No one wanted to listen to this man's fate.
I started seeing people who did not hate.
They smiled and enjoyed the day they'd been given.

I felt all alone with my hate.
As I walked home with sorrow great,
I decided I would not accept hate as my fate.
I will choose another way this day.

No more Hatred Club for me.
I joined the Happy Club as all can see.

Hate…it will destroy you!

HIDE

This tear in my eye is for you.
As I sit alone in this place so blue.
I looked across to the other side
And saw a girl that I could hide.

Her smile was so sweet as I stared.
I made her think that I really cared.
She came to me with her hand held out and we walked side by side.
I took her hand and we searched for a place to hide.

To my surprise, she shed a tear
Saying, "I've been looking for you many a year.
Alone, I've been without a friend," she cried.
"Until I saw you smiling from the other side."

"Please, do not hurt me with foolish pride.
I'm not someone you can hide.
I knew somehow I would find you here.
And that you could be someone to hold so dear."

"You were there in my last night's dream.
It came from someone so supreme
Please don't give up, for I care how you feel.
I'll touch you now and make you real."

I started out to find a girl to hold nigh.
One who I could use to satisfy
This manly pride that I possess,
And then walk away from my recess.

Foolish I am to think that I could use someone for my own pride
Thinking I'd find a girl I could use and then hide,
Just because she was from the other side.
My eyes were opened to care for the girl who now I couldn't hide.

An angel I saw with wings of white
And a door that opened to her heart.
Now we are one to never part.
Just two people from the other side.

JESUS CAME TO SHOW US LOVE

Jesus came to show us love
And now it shines from above.
The wonder of his birth will always be
A miracle for all to see.
Help us master, to show love too
For that is what our lives must do.
His face can shine through us for sure
Our smile with love, the perfect cure.
Don't let us waste our days, our time,
Good we must do so love won't decline
So shed a tear of joy today.
Get up and go the Lord's own way.
Love this day and do not fear.
Yesterday is gone, tomorrow is near.
The advent star is shining still,
If we but follow in his will

The BABE so sweet in the manger scene,
Shows us all GOD's love can mean.
He bring us joy, hope, and peace.

His love

Love for us will never cease…
Lord… Let us each day treat others with love

LISTEN

Listen, my friend, for the words to come.
You will hear them from the mighty tongue.

It is hard to listen to the words that are said.
They seem to pass right through my head.

I would rather talk and drown them out,
Than hear the words from another's mouth.

Why is it I close my ears when another tries to speak?
Do I think their words less than mine or somehow weak?

Do I not wish to hear what is being said to me?
Maybe I think I can't stop to hear for I'm so busy.

If I do not listen then how can I learn?
I need to hear to learn and hopefully wisdom discern.

We must stop to listen to those who have something to say.
It will ease our path as we go on our way.

None of us can possibly know it all,
We should pause to listen to both great and small.

Your heart will be thankful that you opened your ears
To listen to the world around you through the years.

It is not easy to learn to listen, but we must.
Like anything, it takes practice and usage, or else it will rust.

Remember to ask God for help as you try to listen,
For he takes time and cares and he is always listening.

Listen...you will hear it!

LOVE

This day is like all other days.
It begins with light.
It ends with night.
How you use today is up to you.
It is your life; you choose what you will do.

Will it be fear or love that guides your day?
I hope you chose love, my dear.
Be brave and love, casting out your fear.
The head will always put you down and keep you low.
But the heart will raise you up and help you grow.

Cast all doubts and fears away.
Tell yourself to see the love in all.
Then your heart will flow like a waterfall.
Crystal clear and pure you'll be,
As your eyes find love in all they see.

So shed a tear of joy today.
Get up and go your way.
Walk straight ahead and do not sway.
You are not alone when you show love.
For I am with you with my love from above.

This is a day like all other days.
Love this day and do not fear.
Yesterday is gone and tomorrow is very near.
Spread your cheer to all you meet.
Watch yourself grow up in love so sweet.

Love, it will make you!

NADIA

Today I went down a long, long road,
To see a girl named Nadia.
I picked her up and held her close.
She smiled at me and whispered,
"Grandpa, I love you so."

The tears from my eyes fell upon her face.
"Grandpa," she said, "Did I make you sad?"

"No, my dear, I shed these tears
Because I am glad to hold you close.
I give you my heart. No one will ever pull us apart.
I give you my love from the depth of my soul,
To help carry you through so you can be bold."

"Let's go for a walk," she said with a smile.
"We'll come back in a little while."

So walk we did on the white-sand shore.
Sharing time for just the two of us.
How could a Grandpa ask for more?
Old I'm getting; I may not be here long.
So I want her to know me before I am gone.

"I have your picture in a beautiful dress.
It will stay by my bed on my nighttime chest.
I'll send you my picture to place in your crib.
We'll hold to each other with the greatest of care.
And never be separated. That I could not bear."

"How lucky I am to have a princess like you.
A beautiful little girl to light up my life.
The day will come when we won't see one another.
I live a long way from you, my dear.
But in my heart you will always be near."

"Grandpa," she said, "When I close my eyes at night,
I'll say a prayer for you before I fall asleep.
Before I go to sleep, I will probably weep."
I said, "Just call my name and I'll be there.
Listen for my whisper as you close your eyes.

We'll always be together. No more goodbyes.
I love you, my dear. Never forget, just whisper."

THE WEAKER MIND

Once, our leaders had minds that were strong.
They led with pride and bravery.
But now they are gone.
Tell me, what went wrong?

The weaker mind shouted loudly,
"You've had your time. Now it's ours.
Get out! Your mind is old.
It's time for something new."

Our leaders gave in to the weaker mind.
They pushed us off and our hearts were sad.
Yes, the power they had was new but bad.
But the weaker mind said, "We are glad."

They thought they knew what was to be.
But they did not care for you and me.
Their thoughts were on their own reward.
So their ways brought chaos and discord.

The weaker mind was wise in their thoughts,
But only wise in their weaker mind.
Their hearts were cold and black.
A touch of grace and good they all lack.

Oh, how I would, if I could, show them true riches.
Help them see their great castles are mere shacks in ditches.
The weaker mind thinks they have it all.
But for me, this way of life is not my call.

God above is the one who makes the plans.
A walk with him helps us understand where humanity stands.
The weaker mind is filled with pride and treasurers.
The stronger mind is filled with peace and love—true pleasures.

Oh, what they've done to our great time.
Our choices have put upon us such great pain.
The weak leader's kin will pay like you and I,
Because their knee they will not bend.

The world was meant to be built on love
Acknowledging all power is from God above.
So pray for the weaker minds and for their good seek.
It will protect your mind too from growing weak.

TODAY I WENT TO CHURCH

Today I went to church, and there left all my sin.
I couldn't wait to get home and tell all my kin.

When I went into this house of glass,
I looked around and saw such class.
A building full of every colored hat and tie,
Suits and dresses and hair piled high.

I walked the aisle to the front row seat.
The choir sang and my heart skipped a beat.
Angels, I thought, is what they must be.
The words they sang were just for me.

My hair was long and my coat was a tatter.
But I didn't think that would matter.
The preacher stood; he looked my way.
I was meant to hear the words he had to say…

"Thank you for coming this lovely day. Judge not your friends.
For you are one. We all are here to talk about sin.
It lives in all, beneath our skin.
Impure are we before we come."

I went to him, in front where he stood by.
He took my hand and asked me, "Why?"
I said, "To lose my sins and be free of my shame."
The people sang, "We're so glad you came."

The pastor said, "Come greet your friend when we conclude."
The harps in heaven played a tune and the angels smiled with gratitude.
So kind they were to me this day.
To a man who had lost his way.

My heart was full of joy as many a stranger became a friend.
Someone said, "Come home with me. Your coat I can mend."
Another asked to feed my soul.
Yet another gave me a drink and some casserole.

Today I went to church to spend time with hearts of gold.
When I got home I told my father of their love so true and bold.
The people in the house of glass,
Never even knew it was me, dear God.

TODAY—TOMORROW—FOREVER

A moment, is all it takes to say, "I love you truly."
A moment, is all it takes to break your heart into.

Today you hold my hand and whisper words of love.
Today your heart is mine. It is a gift from above.
Today your eyes are blue, with rays of love shining through.
Today there is no doubt that you feel the same as me.
Today our hearts are locked as one and the angels hold the key.
Today our hearts are full of glee.

But…

Tomorrow there'll just be me.

From over there you caught a stare and left me feeling bare.
Your love was gone when you got home.

Tomorrow will be the saddest day.
Tomorrow no words of love I'll hear you say.
Tomorrow my heart will no longer sing to the tune of angels' wings.
Tomorrow I'll start to live alone, finding out where I now belong.
Tomorrow will be long because of your goodbye.

But…

Tonight I'll hang my head in prayer—not for me but for you.

I will not run and hide, just because you were not satisfied.
My head I'll lift high as I search the night sky.

And…

Forever, as I walk life's path, I'll shed a tear for time that's past.
Forever, I'll accept the mold that that God has cast.

TRUTH

Most every man will tell you, "Every word I speak is true."

His head will tell him to speak that way.
For his truth is what he knows, therefore what he knows he will say.

His knowledge is of that which he has been told.
And so he utters his words ever so bold.

It is every man's right to speak his mind.
But others have different minds that form from what they see and find.

It is easy for a man to think that all people should think as he does.
And therefore anyone who does not fall in line must be enemies or foes.

So what is truth? Do we really know?

Search for the truth and it will be found.
Speak the truth with what we know to everyone around.

The truth spoken will not hurt, as long as it does not scar one's fellow man. Untruthful words are meant to harm, and often uttered as a yarn.

True words as we know them will lift us up and do good for all.
While untrue words will tear us down and cause others and self to fall.

Be bound to tell the truth for someone is listening to every word.
You know that is the truth from what you've said and heard.

Do not speak until you know your words are right,
And then surely your future will be bright.

Your heart will guide you to say what is good and just.
Truth is not a choice; it is a must.

Truth…it makes you!

POEMS

BY THE TWO

There was a time that I recall,
When I was loved by both of you.

But now it seems you know me not.
Whatever the reason, it seems I forgot.

Often I wonder how this could be.
For you both hold a key to my happiness.

Do you not know how sad I am?
Do you not know how sad I am?

Why, I wonder.
Is this a time of punishment set on me?
Is there a sin of mine you can't forget?
Or, maybe it's a right, misunderstood.

I long for the time I had it all.
For I know you two were there before the fall.

Judge me now, if you wish.
But that will not fill the hole in my heart.
Love me now, if you wish.
And my heart will no longer cry.
Punish me now, if you wish.
But don't tell me goodbye.

The bond between us can never be broken.
Only the heart, but it can be mended.

Upon ourselves we bring the pain,
That saps the soul and kills the spirit.

We feel so smart when we judge,
But the love we lose when we hold a grudge.

I feel all alone.
Tears will fall from my eyes today.
Just as they did yesterday.
No one cares, but me I guess.

Hope I must have to carry on.
If I stop, I will surely die.

Judge, I will not do.
Grudge, I will not hold.

God made me to love, and so I will.
My wrongs have been put away,
Yet, a shadow in the light lingers still.
Maybe they are not wrongs.
But rights, misunderstood.

BYGONES

Bygones must go, they cannot linger.
If they are in your heart, they will only hinder.

So put them aside and yearn for the offender.
One can offend, but two will mend.

Call your friend and say, "It's not all your fault."
I was wrong and I got caught.
I wanted to blame someone like you.

Everyone thought I was so good and perfect,
But I lied to my Lord and told an untrue.
Now, I'm all alone and oh so blue.

I would like to hear the angels' harp once more.
Please grant me my wish, and maybe I'll score
With you and my Lord and live a little more.

I thought I was smart to blame someone else.
It was easy to do, for I had the ear of the crowd.
I was so foolish but oh so proud.

To tell the tale, I even took a bow.
So away I went with my head held high.
Prancing along under the starry sky.

I knew I had done wrong, but no one would know.
Let her suffer the pain, while I gain the fame.
I need it more than my friend I'd deceived.
But what have I received?

As I thought on this, the night became dark and fear filled my body.

I looked up into the sky. No stars could I see.
The moon hid its face behind a very dark cloud.
My spirit lost its gusto and all of a sudden I was not proud.

Then a voice out of the dark cried, "What have you done?"
"You slandered your friend. What you said was untrue."

As I tried to sleep that dark, dark night,
I kept telling myself that it would be all right.
But wrong I was, for I didn't sleep at all.
I knew in my heart, I was in for a fall.

I told myself I could handle the storm,
It's the best for me, but a doubt began to form.

Why did I do this? She meant no harm.

In the morning light, I knew I had to do what was right.
I went to her house and banged on her door.
A voice inside said, "Go away. I don't love you anymore."
So I sat on the steps and cried.

After awhile, my friend sat down by my side.
She looked at me in my deep despair.
I told her at once I would tell all the truth.

But she said, "We will do it together."
"Remember it takes one to offend, but it takes two to mend."

Bygones must go, they cannot linger.

EARLY MORN

As I awoke before the dawn,
And lay awake with thoughts all my own,
My mind drifted back to another time.
To things I thought I had left behind.
Sadness filled my heart this early morn.

As I thought of two girls that left me alone.
I asked my Lord, "Why did they go?"
"What did I do to deserve this hurt?
I pray each day that they will return,
And I have hope until the sun goes down.
Then I think I'm just a clown.
They don't care if I'm around.

My God I asked, "How can this be?"
I stood by them like a giant tree.
My heart is bound with love for them.
As I shed my tears in the early morn,
I felt the pain of being alone.
Then I drifted back to sleep,

As I slept, I received a message, I believe from above.
Jesus said, "I know you are hurting, but it came from me."
"Look what I had to go through.
I was a man, the same as you.
My sadness was great, and I wondered just like you.
But God gave me a break, he made me his son."

Jesus said, "Trust me, my son, and you will be just fine.
There are many and they are your kind.
Look beyond your sight, you are not blind.
You can see me now as I hang from the cross.
I've been looking for you to come take me down.
You see I'm still bound and I feel your pain."

"Here is my Spirit in this white dove.
It will fly with you wherever I send you,
So you will know I've taught you to love,
I've taught you to care and I've told you that I'll always be there.
We are two of a kind. You and I.
Both trying to be and do what God has called us here for.

So, my son, enjoy the pain.
If you do you will have great gain.
Look beyond your sight and see my face.
Now your heart will have might and your pain will show love.
With you will be my dove,
That only you can see.

As I awake again before the dawn,
My face is wet from many a tear.
My heart is full of greater pain.
And I realize my tears were pure and crystal clear.
My heart is full of the greatest joy.

That early morn I heard the flutter of a dove's wings.
"All of this for me?" I thought.
Yes!
Jesus came down to me that early morn,
Just to say…
You and me.

FEELING LOW

I woke up this morning feeling kind of low.
It was all because I was no longer a beau.
I crawled out of bed and put on my rags.
Cried in my coffee and played tag with my biscuit.
I looked out the window; it was stormy and wet.
How was I to get through this dark day?
I had hurt someone, but I didn't think it was much.

I combed my hair and grabbed my car keys,
Went to the garage with no place to go.
I opened the door and there it sat.
My car, my friend. It wouldn't leave me flat.
I opened the door and crawled inside.
Trusty as always, he said, "Fasten your seat belt."

I obeyed without question and felt secure.
I keyed the ignition and listened for the purr.
It sounded kind of flat. I thought, where is my cat?
Then I turned on the computer and it came to life.
I asked it, "Where are we going today?"

"I don't know about me, but
It looks like you're going down the road to Hell.
I know I have to take you there if you choose to go.
From the shape you are in, I guess we don't have a choice."

I was shocked to the bone and felt all alone.
The world was not my friend and now my car was telling me so.
"It's getting hotter outside. I don't like this road," he said,
"And I don't like dark brown toast."

I said, "Not to worry, my friend, we have air conditioning.
And I'm cool as a toad. Just take another road."
"I'm in charge," I said with pride. "I programmed you, you have no choice.
You belong to me, so do what I say."

I felt so powerful as I clutched the wheel.
Then the air conditioner stopped and the cool was gone.
I knew I was in trouble, so I pushed on the peddle.
Too my surprise the engine stopped, and I asked my car, "What are you doing?"

"Look," he said, "I told you once that I don't like dark brown toast.
I know you think you are the most, but it's hot out here."
The storms got violent, and the rain came down.
I began to fear the car was right. You see I don't like dark brown toast either.
I asked my Lord, "Where did I go wrong?"
He said, "You took a wrong turn, that's why you are alone."
"Well, Lord," I said, "Where is that road?"
"It's in your head," he said, "You have no shine, you left it behind."

The storm got worse, and it started to snow.
I could not see very far ahead.
I asked the Lord, "Where is the switch? Soon, I won't see at all.
For darkness will cover me and cause me to fall."

"I'll be lost without hope, and I will never see you at all.
And if this motor cranks, I'll be shot into Hell."
I tried to turn on my lights, but the battery was dead.
I thought for sure I would be next.

Then the Lord said, "I will give you light if you want it."

"Of course I want it, for I can't see."

"I know," he said, "But your light is not up to me."

"Why," I said, "aren't you in charge?"

"Yes," he said, "but you already have the light."

"Where, Lord? I'm not shining. It is dark down here with no light at all."

"Turn on your heart to others," he said, "Love them and be true to everyone."

"Thank you, Lord, this I will do."

So he switched on my light, and I began to glow.
I looked outside and there was no snow.
The storm was gone, and the sun was peeping through.
The car started up and said, "Let's head for home."

As we traveled along, I waved at the crowds, and the car honked its horn.
We found a joy like we were reborn.
I said to the car, "Thanks for taking me home."
"No, thank you," he said.
Neither one of us like dark brown toast.

I DON'T THINK I EVER WILL

I don't think I ever will, find a love to call my own.
Someone to say, "I'm glad you're here."
Someone to hold me near.

I live my life alone and wait, but fear it is too late.
My hope is gone for I have no love.
I don't think it ever will, come my way.

My life I gave to others the best I could.
Some said, "Thank you." Others passed me by.
I've loved a lot. I've lost a lot.
But in the end, I've won the battle.

The Spirit within my soul is strong.
It lifts me up each day.
It teaches me how to forgive.
It teaches me how to love.
It takes my hand as I walk through each day, and says,
"I will be with you as long as you have courage."

As I sit here in this early morning,
I feel the gentle breeze sent to cool my heart.
I plan my day the best I can,
Knowing my spirit will not let me down.

If I fail today, it will be my own fault.
I have no one else to blame.
I will face today with courage.
I will not let myself down.
For I have found a strength from within.

If I don't ever find a love to call my own, I will not weep.
I will keep a steady pace and give what I can to all I greet.
I don't think I ever will, stop giving all the love I can.

I WANT TO THANK YOU

I want to thank you for the things you said, and
The lack of love, we didn't share in our bed.
I want to thank you for no tender touch or
Loving kiss to calm my soul.

Sometimes I would give a hug though I knew I was being bold.
But I needed it so, even though you were so cold.

To please you, was never.
To shame you, was always.
So I was told by you.

I want to thank you for my hospital stays,
Where I learned there was love in the world.
We all had been mistreated, though none knew why.
Our only goal was to survive.

We had a little cry and hugs from those there.
Love between us to share.
I learned to care.
I learned I was not a bear.

You were sick, I knew all along.
I tried to help you, but you wore me to the bone.

I wanted run.
I wanted to stay.
Most of all, I wanted you well.
So...stay I did, for a very long spell.

A monster I became to your blue eyes.
So many times I should have said my goodbyes.
Walk out? I couldn't, for I loved you so.
I prayed each night, "Lord, help her, please."

You hated me so.
I knew it all, so well.
You hated yourself more
But you didn't know why.

You told me that I was supposed to make you happy.
I wish I could, but that was up to you.
I want to thank you for the hardships I bore.
I made it through and now I'm wiser to the core.

My spirit is strong.
It was all for a purpose.
I don't know why.
I trust, for I am not shy.

Tears I shed as I lay on my bed.
No regrets.
I'm happy for all that I did.
I would do it again if I thought it would help.

I want to thank you for the wisdom I gained.
Now that I'm gone, you have no one to blame.
Stop and think as you look in the mirror.
You wanted something better than you had at home.

I hope you found it now that you are all alone.
I am all alone, but I won't be for long.
I want to thank you for the happiness I found.

IF YOU EVER LOVED SOMEONE

Have you ever loved someone…like I love someone?
Have you ever needed someone…like I need someone?
Has your heart ever cried…like my heart cries?
Have you ever missed someone…like I miss someone?

Did you ever need someone to explain love to you?
Have you ever forgiven someone you love?
If you have not…you have never loved.

When you listen to your heart, where your love lies,
You will find your answers to loves great questions.

For the heart holds love and understanding.
It will make you sad.
It will make you glad.

You must learn to love through,
The tears, and
The smiles.

The heart may be broken, but…someday it will mend.

Do not let bad thoughts cloud your heart with doubt and fears.
Think of what you had and loved for years and years.

Look into the eyes of your children
And you will know you did right.

Let your heart now cry and your love will grow deep.

Do what you should do in life, but never stop loving.
The more love you give, the more love you get.

So love with your heart and don't try to understand.
There is a beginning to love we know,
But only your heart knows when love ends.

So stay true to your heart through,
Tears, and
Smiles.

Know how lucky you are to have a great love.

LET ME HEAR YOUR HEARTBEAT

Let me hear your heartbeat.
Let me hold you close to mine.
Now that we are older,
It takes both hearts to live.

When your heart was gone,
Mine was left all alone.
Somehow you felt you would like to live without me.
It was hard for me to see,
Your love for me was gone.

Now you live alone in a place I used to call home.
Your heart is beating alone without the beat of mine.
I hope your heart grows stronger as you sit there all alone.
My deepest wish for you is that you find what you are looking for.

As I sit here in this place I now call a home,
I find my heart is beating strong, but I am all alone.
I may have lost a heart that used to beat with mine,
But my heart will survive to beat again for someone else.

Yes, my heartbeat's alone,
But that won't be for long.
For today, I looked around and found that I was not all alone.
There were other hearts beating that looked for a heart like mine.

Someday I will hear a heartbeat and hold it close to mine.
It will not be your heartbeat,
For it will be a true heartbeat,
One that loves to be felt close.

Now that we are older,
It takes two hearts to live.

MY MISTAKE

I went out this morning with no joy in my heart.
I knew I had been coy and I would have to pay.
My heart has been heavy; I know I've done wrong.
Sometimes the boy is afraid to do his part.

She was walking down the street,
When I saw in her eyes that I had been beat.
She said, "Is there something you haven't told me?"

I stopped in my tracks as my heart said, I told you so.
What was I to do?

"The truth will do. It will save your soul," said he.

But, Lord, it's just me, and I am in love.

"You are not alone my son.
Tell her the facts and I will consider you.
Don't look to me for help.
You must do it yourself and then we will see.
Beg for her forgiveness then you may beg for mine."

But, Lord, I'm afraid. She might walk away.
Then I would be like a lump of clay,
I'd return to dust, and
The wind would blow me away.

"My son, you must show courage.
Do not sway and let me down too.
I need you, as maybe does she."

I told her the truth with a tear in my eye,
And waited for the sound of the wind.

She said, "I understand, but you should not have…"

We talked for a little while as we walked down the street.
She was kind and understanding, but I still felt beat.
I told her I would never repeat,
If she would only forgive so I could live.
My confession to her lightened my burden.

The Lord smiled and said, "Well done, my son.
Walk free now and I will consider."
She turned to me with those beautiful brown eyes.
Spread her wings and flew into the sky.
She hovered above and then said, "Goodbye."

Then with a big smile, she whispered,
"I'll be around when you settle your score."

Then she disappeared from my view.
I felt sad but my heart was lighter.

I had heard another whisper,
"Now, finish your task and I might give you the key to her heart,
If only you will do your part."

"Thank you, Lord," my heart said with a song.
I knew it wouldn't be long.

NO ONE IN HEAVEN
WAITS FOR ME

There will be no one in heaven to wait for me,
For all my loves had other loves.
They say they love me, but then they sigh and speak of their love
before they knew me.

So I sit and listen and wonder why it is my lot to sit and cry.
As I sit alone in the dark, I know I have to play this part.
I wipe the tears from my eyes and try to understand.

I say to myself, "I'll do the best I can if I am meant to live this way.
I'll hold my head high and
walk so tall no one will know my thoughts at all."

I will care, and I will love and wait for the Spirit that comes from
above.
I suppose all I did in life just wasn't good enough to please the Master
who sits on high.
Sometimes I think I feel him nigh, but who can tell on such dark
nights.

When my loves get there, I hope they find their loves that wait for
them.
I will bare this lonely pain that lives within my heart.
No one will know but he and I, as I live my life both day and night.

Deep joy I know as I take flight and spread his love with all my
might.
For he is love and love is he, and I know I will be with him some day.
But he is not ready to call me home; I have tasks left to do.

I only feel this way because I am mortal,
With wisdom that's not too great, I fear.
But someday I'll wonder why I felt this way.
On that day when it will all become clear.

Everyone needs someone to love and say to them, "I'll be waiting there."
As I pondered these words of care, my mind was opened and I heard a voice.
"Do not despair for I am there. I am waiting for you."

The voice said, "You must love and trust and do my good.
Let my Spirit control your mood.
Go about your daily tasks with my great love for all you touch and see.
For I am you and you are me."

"When I am ready I'll call you home and I'll be waiting just for you."
My great love in heaven waits for me.

PEOPLE I USED TO KNOW

As I think today of times long ago,
My mind returns to the people I used to know.
A flood of water washes my face,
As I feel their love from a faraway place.

The joy of today that fills my soul is made supreme
By a great dream of people I used to know.

My kin were my greatest friends.
Their heart was mine as well as theirs.
They shared their love and did not compare.

As they patted my head and said, "Be a good boy, my dear."
They taught me to be a fellow with pride.
But if I was bad, they would tan my hide.

A life like mine was for everyone I thought.
But as I looked around, some others were not.
I wondered why as I asked them to play.

Why did they frown on such a lovely day?
They had no Dad around, not even to mow the hay.
No kin to pat them on the head and say, "Be a good boy."

I wondered at night before I fell asleep,
Why I had a mom, dad, and lots of kin.
But others did not have these special friends.

I made up my mind to share friends
With all who had no Dad at home,
Or Kin to call their own.

As I grew older and started to school,
More friends I had each day in the class.

Days and years rolled by so fast.
But I never forgot the friends of my past.
I learned so much from all of them.

As I grew older, I lost some friends,
But I could always find new ones if I looked around.
There were always people alone with a frown.

I looked up above and asked, "Why, my Lord?"
For I had been taught to pray each day.
I made up my mind to be a friend to all who were around.
I wanted them to be happy,
And just like me, have a loving pappy.

As I grew older with children of my own,
I'm thankful for the people I used to know who taught me to care.
I hope that someday, like me, my children will say,
"I learned to care from Mom, Dad, and the people I used to know."

THANK GOD FOR
MY NEW LOVE

Thank God for my new love.

My prayers were answered with beauty and grace.
He sent me an angel from above.
Her eyes still my soul and her touch makes me tremble.
When we are together, I feel we become as one.

As I hold her tight, an angel smiles, touches us, and says…
"This is God's gift to you. May both hearts cherish the other, for the
two have become one."

I fear I can lose my way;
Following my heart is not an easy task.
A higher power guides my day.
So who is to say how I should act?

Some might ask,
"How do you know what is right or wrong as you look for love from
day to day?"

I say,
"Don't look too hard, let it find you. Then you will know what is
right for you."

My life has been good.
I believed in serving my time, paying my dues, and accepting the
strife.
Perhaps I was right, or perhaps I was wrong.
Who is to say for sure as our paths in life we tried tread along.

Thank God for my new love.
I don't know if she feels the same way.
Does her heart really join with mine?
Only she knows what her heart does say.

I hope her heart is saying...

Thank God for my new love.

THE FRONT PORCH

As I sit here on this front porch,
The sun shines down on shades of green.

I close my eyes and fall back in time,
Although I know it is just a dream.
I am once again in another place,
A place called home—so long ago.

I looked out from my front porch,
As the sun shined down on shades of green.

It was here I learned to love and pray,
Always thinking tomorrow will be another day.
There was not much food, and lots of work.
Not much money, but we could somehow pay.

I knew I was loved from the day I was born;
I could see it in my mother's eyes every morn.
Some mothers teach their children of other things,
But I was lucky to have been taught of love.

Love is the hardest way to live for some.
I don't know why; it seems so troublesome.
I have lived my days with love in my heart,
And filled my nights with prayer.

I do not know if this was right or wrong,
It was what I was taught before I was grown.
I did not know then what I was learning
Would shape my life and guide my heart's yearning.

My days would be filled with love,
And my nights would be filled with prayer.

As I sit here on this front porch,
The sun shines down on shades of green.

With my eyes full of tears,
And my heart full of love,
I cry for a while, but without any shame.
For what I've become, I am to blame.

As I pondered these thoughts,
I felt it was time for my dream to end.
I knew I must get back to where it began.
But I sat a little longer on the old front porch.

I wondered, "What kind of man have I become?"
Then drifted back once more to the front porch.
For there, everything seemed real again.
Though I still wondered what kind of man I'd become.

My answer came when I heard a voice,
"Dad, where are you?" calling from inside.
My eyes filled with tears, and my heart filled with love,
I cried awhile, and I was not ashamed.

Once again, I sit here alone on this front porch,
As the sun shines down on shades of green.

THE MEANING OF LIFE

Life has no meaning...you are born and grope around until you die.

We're told to love and care...just to have our heart broken.

No one loves you...they need you.

"Do what I say! Your thoughts mean nothing."

I may listen, just to be nice.
You live in the past; you want me there too.

The ones who die young?
They're the lucky ones.
They go to sleep with peace as a pillow.

Follow the pack.
Do what you are told.
Stay in line.
Don't cause a ripple.

If you want to be loved...it will be on my terms.

You are told you have choices...I'll tell you which ones.

If you choose the one you like?
No pleasure will be yours.

Life has no purpose for those who will to please.
Good is no thought to those that demand.

For those who like to love will find they have no future.
It will be taken away by those who have no caring.

"Why am I here?" you may ask, but don't bother.
No one is interested.

Life does not care for those who stand up.
Too many around are saying, "Sit down. Shut up."

I have no clue as to why I am here.
A tree will grow best if no one comes near.

So…why a human race?
I rest my case.

THE OLD WILLOW TREE

There is an old willow tree in our backyard.
It stands alone, out near the barn.
It has no friend, no tree nearby.
It stands alone under the open sky.

It seemed happy for someone to come by,
And touch a limb or pluck a leaf.
I watched the old willow tree for many years.
It never failed to show its love.

Old Willow weathered the storms and harsh winds.
I stood alone watching the tree with its mighty trunk and giving limbs.
I pondered how strong it was, yet gentle too.
I wished someday I could be like that old tree.

I soon left home and the old willow tree.
I went into the world to see what I could be.
I found me a job I liked and worked hard with all my might.
But I missed my home each day and night.

My work was good; I had been taught by the best.
Mom taught me to pray.
Dad taught me to work.
And the old willow tree taught me to stand.

Years went by and my family was now more than one.
I was a dad myself and so proud when I looked at my children.
With tears in my eyes, I understood love.
So I thanked the heaven above.

I took their little hands and walked down the street,
Showing them off to everyone we would meet.
Each day I'd go to work, glad to strive to master the task.
Problems I had most every day, but I made it through doing as they ask.

I learned so much from my mom and dad.
It was all good. There was no bad.
I worked my way up, from job to job.
My best I would give from place to place.

You see, it wasn't up to me;
Someone else was calling the shots.
But then my stint was over; my time had passed.
I look back knowing my life has been blessed.

I weathered it all through the storms and the wind
I stood strong with outstretched giving limbs.
The tree beckoned me back, curious to see.
If it was still standing, just like me.

There it was, the old willow tree was still standing.
There was no barn.
There was no yard.
There was only the old willow tree standing alone.

THIS IS THE DAY THE LORD HAS MADE

This is the day the Lord has made.
I must take it as my own.

As I look out from this bedroom,
The sky is dark and full of gloom.
My eyes see no rain though the streets are wet.
I'm grateful all my needs are met.

The trees are budding and the flowers bloom.
My heart is beating with a heavenly tune.
The earth is grooming itself once again,
So that you and I may shout with glee.
I leave my house to walk among the menagerie.

I watch the dew kiss every flower with new life.
I want to touch every petal I see.
I sing to them and they sing to me.
Together we make a symphony.

I find a rock to sit upon and pray.
I would like to stay here all day.
But I knew work was calling after a spell.
It was time to walk on; I could tell.

So I say goodbye to the flowers and the trees,
To enter another world of friends, all busy as bees.
Each of them has been given this day, too.
But some can't see, they have no clue,
That this is the day the Lord has made.

I move among the smiles and frowns shown.
Hoping each will make this day their own.
We all need the Spirit who guides us along.
Though we like to think we make our way,
As we move through life, while we decay.

I wish that each could have been with me,
As I walked among God's beautiful menagerie.
If they did, I'm sure they would all agree,
And shout with praise, along with me—
This is the day the Lord has made!

TODAY I LOST A ROSE

Today I lost a rose.
A rose that was a bright, bright red.
It started as a bud that grew throughout the years.

Once it was in full bloom with many beautiful petals.
But today, a strong wind swept up through the valley and blew the petals apart.

I stood and watched the petals fly away, but they did not fall on land or sea.
They drifted upward toward the Heavens, dancing as they moved with the wind.

I watched with delight with tears in my eyes.
For I knew I would never see the rose again.

While I was watching, the petals came back together.
And to my surprise, it became a beautiful rose once more.

Time had caused the petals to fade,
But now it was bright, bright red again.

I saw a door swing open and I watched as my rose went through heaven's gate.
I cried with wonder at what I saw as the gate took my rose away.

Then I saw a great white glow from inside the gate.
It was my rose, that scarlet rose, bright inside of heaven's door.

As I watched it change, it turned white as snow
It was shining bright upon a hill inside of heaven.

It seemed to look back at me and say, "I started out as a bright red rose.
Although the color faded as time passed by, I knew someday I would be bright red again."

"My red glow turned bright white as I came through heaven's gate.
I have not gone away. I've only moved here to shine upon this hill inside of heaven's gate."

"My light will shine for you, my dear, so do not lose sight of my bright white light.
It will not dim until you come, and then together we will make a bright, bright light inside
heaven's gate."

WHAT MAKES YOUR STAR SHINE?

Down deep in everyone's heart is a star that wants to go to heaven.

The star starts out as a little dot, so small.
So tiny no one can see it at all.

We spend our days trying to make that dot grow.
We hope one day it will be a bright star and white glow.

When it's just a dot, it's black but grows bigger day and night.
It can stay black or can slowly change to white.

A star stays black if the heart is cold, thinking only of itself.
A star cannot change to white if its heart is selfish and uncaring.

Heart stars only change to white when the heart begins to care for others.
When it gives its love and understanding to someone beside itself.

When you love someone else, you find that you love yourself more too.
Your heart feels good about what you are doing as you love others.

When your heart feels good then your star begins to grow
And it slowly starts turning from black to white.

Your star only grows when you do things that please it.
Do something nice for someone each day and your star glows bright white.

Doing good to others starts with your own family who teaches you love and understanding,
If you endure in loving and caring and doing good, your star will grow brighter.

Very few things in life come easy but be thankful for this.
The more hardships you overcome, the more your star will shine bright.

Don't go through life with a black star. Use the time you have to turn it white as snow.
As for me, I want my star to be a bright white glow.

When my daughters look up at the night sky full of stars, too many to count,
I want them to say, "That bright white star over there is Dad!"

And how will they know that star in heaven is me?
They will know because its white glow shins bright for them to see.

WORTHLESS

Worthless.
Have you ever felt worthless?
Then you have walked in my shoes.

You have cried my tears.
Your heart has ached with pain.
You have lost your love.

The sparkle in her eyes lost their glow of love.
Her touch became demanding.
Her skin lost its silky feel.

She began to want more than I could give.
She judged me by her standards, knowing I would fail,
No matter how hard I tried.

Her life became a chore.
I wondered why.
Each day I could see her real life slipping away.

She chose her own style,
Without concern for me,
Or consideration of her family.

As she lost the love for herself,
She began to wonder if I loved her at all.
Did anyone love her?

She created her own unhappiness,
Blaming everyone else,
Blaming anyone else, for her feelings.

Yes, at times she made me feel worthless.
She did a good job of this.
But my love was stronger than my anger.

Although I was worthless in her eyes,
I knew I could be something to someone,
If I believed in myself and kept love alive in my heart.

Worthless.
Have you ever felt worthless?
Don't let it get you down.

Hold your head up high.
Put a smile on your face.
And be thankful.

Someone out there needs you.
Don't let them down.
Don't lose that glow in your eyes.

Just because someone stopped loving you,
Doesn't mean you stopped living.
You have a lot of love to give—don't let it die.

Worthless?
Yes. I felt worthless that day.
She thought she had won and was pleased with herself.

But time ruled against her.
She believed real pleasures came to her,
When she was in someone else's arms.

Yes, she thought she had won.
But she had really lost.
She lost true love, my love—more than could be found elsewhere.

PROSE

EVEN A WEED

Even a weed becomes a flower,
If it is looked at with love.

They call me a weed.
I don't know why.
When I hear them talk.
I just want to cry.

My feelings get hurt, and my pride takes a blow.
Don't they see, all I want to do is grow.

If they would just leave me alone,
And stop cutting me to the bone.
I would show them my charm.
My heart is big, just like theirs.

I am beautiful inside you see.
I dream of having a growing spree.
A chance is all I need.
Just like a flowering seed.

Why is a flower so loved by all?
Even I admire its beauty.
Oh, how I wish someone would see me
And call me cutie.

When I look at a flower, I have to smile.
When a flower looks at me, it seems to revile.
So I asked, "Flower, why do you not like me?
I want to be your friend."

I wave at her and say, "My leaves are dark green,
And they have such a pretty sheen."
But she frowns and says, "Why didn't you stay in the ground?
No one loves you. Just look around."

She says, "They love my bloom and they give me a smile.
Even the bees come buzzing near.
Why are you here? You are only a weed.
You are not needed, don't you see?"

But God made me. There must be a reason.
I'm proud of my green and shine through the season.
I determine I will not go away.
No matter what the flower will say.

"Oh, you talk so brave," said the flower that bloomed.
"But in this garden of love, you've no chance. You are doomed.
They will cut you to the bone one day.
And then you will simply fade away."

But I believe I have a beauty that someone will find.
If I keep choosing to be kind.
The flower may have her blooms, but I have my light.
And someday someone will hold me tight.

One day, I looked up and saw the flower had lost her bloom.
She looked just like me, a weed, no smile, just doom and gloom.
But unlike mine, her leaves were not green and shiny.
I heard her cry as she faded away, pale and whiney.

I reached out my leaf and caught her tear.
I felt so sorry for this flower that did not want me near.
The flower looked up and asked me, "How can you care?
I was so rude and mean, so unfair."

"Yes," I said, "I could have learned to hate from you.
But I made a choice to be kind and true.
I soaked in the light and grew from its love and care.
I'm so full of light, I've got plenty to share."

The flower hung her head and said, "I'm only a flower without a bloom.
Now I'm just like a weed that no one will love."
But I smiled and said, "Stop shedding your tears,
And give me your leaf. You've got plenty more years."

"We will be friends and I'll show you my light.
You are still beautiful in this weed's sight."
The flower protested, "How can you love me all faded and bare?"
I sighed, "Because I have the light and I know how to care."

Even a weed becomes a flower,
If it is looked at with love.

FUZZY NUT

Fuzzy Nut was a squirrel who lived way up north where it was very cold.
He lived with his papa and mama, but his papa died, and his mama was old.
They lived high up in a big tree in a great big hole.

In their hole, they were just as cozy and warm as they could be.
But they both missed papa who had been set free.
Mama said he now lived in Squirrel Villa in a happy tree.
She said someday she would join him, but for now lived with me.

One day Mama said it was time for me to become a squirrel man.
I had to go out and gather the nuts we needed for food.
As she looked at me with a tear in her eye,
My heart began aching and I started to cry.

But away I went to find us some nuts down below.
I knew where to look, but they were covered with snow.
It was very cold, and I shivered and shook for my fur was thin.
Frost was on my paws, my nose, and even my chin.

There were no nuts I could find down below,
So I went home with my head held low.
I told my mama that I had failed and come home because I was so cold.
She said, "Don't worry, my squirrel man. You were very bold."

Mama said as I go out in the cold my fur will grow.
So each day I went out to find nuts for Mama in the cold snow.
I watched as my fur grew thick, even around my feet.
I was as happy as I could be, for I found nuts for Mama and me.

Each day I came home with my head held high.
My Mama would pat my head, store the nuts, and smile all the while.
Each night as I went to bed I slept sound with my mind at rest,
For, Mama was proud of her squirrel man and I knew I had done my best.

One day Mama said, "You have earned your thick fur all by yourself.
And look at all the nuts you found stored here on our shelf.
I think I'll call you Fuzzy for that is what my squirrel man has become.
I'll carve 'Fuzzy' on a nut and place it on the mantle in honor of where all the nuts came from.

So Fuzzy I am and Fuzzy I'll be for everyone to see.
My heartbeats with pride inside this squirrel man, all cozy and warm inside my big tree.

OLD HANDS

As I sit here in this old swing.
I think of all the memories it brings.

There once was laughter that rang in the air,
And many words spoken with love and care.
But the hand writing these words, now walks with a cane,
The fingers crooked, wrinkled, and suffering pain.

Sometimes the pain is more than I can bare.
Though, I'm grateful all the fingers are still there.
My old hands don't make me sad; no I'm rather glad.
For I know things are not all that bad.

I look down at my old feet.
I bet they could still walk a beat.
They push this old swing as I rock back and forth.
Happiness flows through me like the wind through the trees.

Then my heart skipped a beat and reminded me to smile.

I touch my old face with my old hands.
The wrinkles are there, lines in deep bands.
They circle my face in an upward turn.
For a smoother face, I begin to yearn.

But my heart skipped a beat and reminded me to smile.

I thought about my old brain.
Some days it is as if it has grown a drain.
A lifetime of learning is mostly gone.
I want to remember all that I have forgotten.

As I try to speak, the words won't come.
It makes me feel worthless, like an old bum.
I wish I could find a plug for the drain,
So I could hang on to what's left of this old brain.

Then my heart skipped a beat and reminded me to smile.

I look out over our garden.
It is so beautiful. We call it our Eden.
There stood an angel to my right
And another to my left, both saying, "It's all right."

I see life's flowing water spilling over the dam.
All things I see seem to speak to me.
The birds are singing and the butterflies winging.
The flowers are blooming and the palms waving.

Then my heart skipped a beat and reminded me to smile.

My years have been many, just like this old swing.
And when I sit here, I feel like a king.

I stop counting years left to look down at my old hands.
Soon they will be playing in angels' bands.
They are still wrinkled and a little pained.
My fingers still crooked, they had not changed.

But one day, the pain will be gone, and the wrinkles too.

Then my heart skipped a beat and reminded me to smile.

OLD SHOE

I am here in the corner, all moldy and musty.
Even my leather is old and crusty.
I am weak and lonely, without another sole.
I need company as I lie here alone.

No one notices that my wrinkles are weeping,
And the lines in my face are extending and deepening.
I once was so proud, to the tip of my toe.
Now I lay helpless wishing for more.

I was bright and shiny as I went on my way.
Now I'm left on the floor to fade and decay.
I did my time, step after step.
Serving, leading, carrying, and giving.

I would give comfort to all placed in my care.
Now I look around and the floor is bare.
They went on their way and left me to die.
They forgot me and all I once did.

In your brand-new soles, you walked out the door.
While I was here to teach you so much more.
Not once did you stop to ask advice from an old sole.
You thought you knew all you needed to know.

But there was much I could and wanted to tell you.
Like when your shine grows dull, all the things you can do.
Secrets of polish and buffing and keeping it bright.
And healing the scares that come with the years.

One day you'll cry, "Will my soles become wrinkled and crusty?"
"Will I be tossed in the comer, to mold and smell musty?"
These are the questions you don't think to ask,
For you are still new and walking new paths.

"Yes, they will!" I wanted to say from my dark hole.
But it's never too late to have a forgiving sole.
I wasn't perfect as I walked the streets.
But I'll share my life lessons to help you walk better.

Easing your burden was my goal deep inside.
But you didn't need me; you tossed me aside.
You felt I should just abide in the comer,
Resting and fading for soon I would die.

My tongue cries, "No! I am not done!"
I can't just rot in a corner; my sole seeks more fun.
Your lack of love for me makes me sad.
So I'm praying for someone to help me belong.

I waited and waited, hoping for a new day.
Nightly I wept tears as my prayers I would say.
Deep in my sole, I knew I would be worn again.
Then it came. A new bottle of polish set by my toe.

I smiled with delight and watched from below.
With love, a hand picked me up and polished my toe.
Now, I walk with love as I pound the street.
And fall asleep each night feeling loved and fulfilled.

My sole was saved by a helping hand that was there all along.
I just had to ask.

SANDY

When I was just a lad, so small,
You could always find me at Grandpa's side.
I don't know why he was so great.
But he was the man that set my fate.

He walked with God along life's path.
All others were just no match.
For in my eyes he stood so tall.
My grandpa was the best of all.

He never knew how I loved him,
Or how I wanted to be his gem.
Early one morn he went away
To a place he'll always stay.

He had done his job, at least with me.
Helped turn me into what I would be.
Love and honor was his game.
He played it daily, no matter the pain.

I owe him today for what he did.
Although I am not a kid from long, long ago,
Love and honor is now my game.
And I will not run and hid when I feel the pain.

I lift my eyes toward the sky.
A gentle breeze cools my face and makes me smile.
I know that Grandpa is there,
Reminding me that he stands with me here.

SOLDIER

A Soldier is a person with pride.
When they have died, many have cried.
As I write these words, my eyes tear and my hands shake.
For Uncle Vonnie, my heart still aches.

I have to stop for a moment, until I can see.
It was long ago that he came to me.
He said goodbye and I knew what was to be.
We both knew it was our last, for God revealed it to him and me.

As I watched him leave for the very last,
I was caught between the present and the past.
I could see myself looking out through the windowpane.
A moment mixed with pride, love, sorrow, and pain.

Off he went to war in his brand-new uniform.
And with him went the hope that the world would reform.
Some time later, two men came to the front door.
They said Uncle Vonnie was with us no more.

As I think of him now in this room where I write,
He is standing beside me here in this night.
I don't know, but I can guess that he loves me still and wants me to
do my best.
I want to tell his story so he can rest.

Please rest, my friend, for you've done your part.
Go now and listen to the angels' harp.
I dedicate this to all who wear the brand-new uniform.
We all know now that the world will not reform.

They march to the beat of the freedom drum.
Giving their lives for the hope of peace to come.
Taps are heard when brave soldiers fall.
They all went up when they heard the call.

I don't know why they are so brave.
So many have wept over their grave.
I would like to understand more if I can.
But I believe it's part of every woman and man.

The desire to protect what God has given us, we admit.
We earned what we have and we're determined to keep it.
Tread lightly any country that wants us to fall.
Our Country we love and it's blessed from above.

To all those who died and all those that cried.
I won't let you down. I'll stand by your side.
I'll wear that uniform if I get the call.
Why? Because I love you best of all.

THE COUNTY SEAT

There once was a boy, a man to be,
Who loved his home and all he could see.
He was master of the land, the birds, and the trees.
He wandered all over from mornin' 'til night,
With glee in his eyes and wonder in his heart.

He thought he would never part from this place that was his.
Until the time he traveled far, all the way to the County Seat.

It was not as much fun as folks said it would be.
The sidewalks were hard on his bare feet.
He wanted to go home before he was beat.
He was with his dad so he didn't stray but said, "Dad, do we have to stay?"

His dad said, "Son, don't be afraid. Just hold my hand. We're doing this together."
So he walked with his dad as he pulled me along.
He said, "Hurry, Son, and then we'll go home."
With those words, he hastened his step.

The people were friendly. They all smiled and asked how we were.
Dad smiled back and said, "Fine, thank you."
Dad looked at me when I did not speak, and said, "Where is your smile?
You must not keep it. Share it with all you meet."

The boy put on his smile as he walked with his dad.
"Remember, Son," said his dad, "you never want to be a sore lad."

They went in a store at the end of the block
To buy some cloth for Mom to sew.
Sister needed a dress. She didn't have but one.
If she had another, she would think she was blessed.

As we left the store, Dad said, "Look at the clock. It's time to go."
We lumbered back down the block to the stables where the horses
were tied.
I crawled on the back and lay on a sack. Dad sat in the seat and said,
"Getty-up!"
The horses responded and went to a gallop.
They pranced along as they headed for home.

There was joy in my heart as I closed my eyes.
I dreamed of the new friends that I met today.
I wasn't afraid anymore, as long as Dad was near.
I did like my visit, but it was so far from home.
I was sure I would never come back again to the County Seat.

THE LAST PEANUT

I am just a nut that lives in the ground.
It's cold and damp and about a foot down.
I have a warm shell that keeps me dry.
But when I was young, I used to cry,
And wonder why I was a nut in the ground.

When I saw my family, I knew I was not alone.
They told me that this is where I belong.
They said I had a family, a large family of nuts in the ground.
Our life was good about a foot down.
We all grew up together through rain and snow.

I worked and played and had high hopes that were swell.
I grew to be plump inside my warm shell.
But once I was grown, I was ready to be on my own.
I knew everything a nut could possibly have known.
I became lonely, for I had withdrawn from my family and friends.

I was too good to be in the ground still.
I wanted to see the world above, experience a thrill.
So I packed my suitcase and kept it near.
I could not bare my home buried down here.

One day, I felt a tug and I knew I was bound to be free.
We flew through the air, my family and me.
We said goodbye with tears in our eyes.
I lost my family when we fell in the bucket with other nuts.

I never knew there were so many nuts living in the ground about a
foot down.

I made new friends as we moved from pot to pot.
We laughed and sang and partied a lot.
Then one day, they gave me a mop and said clean, no ifs and or buts.
They put me to work like all ordinary nuts.
But I felt I was too good to handle a mop, so they put me in a bag instead.

I made new friends with the nuts in the bag,
And felt so smart that I'd dropped the mop and cleaning rag
We laughed and sang and partied a lot.
Until the day the bag was opened and we all whispered, "What?"

One by one they took us out.
I had to find out what this was all about.
I peeped up over the bag top.
I knew from what I saw my life would soon stop.
But I was okay, for I had been a good nut and was ready to go.

Now I'm in a different place filled with nuts without their shells.
Around their nut necks, hang little bells.
They have little wings so they fly around.
These were no ordinary nuts that lived in the ground.
They must be heavenly nuts, and then so I must too.

As I pondered this, a big nut appeared and gave me a smile.
He touched me and I grew wings. I was not afraid all the while.
For I was no longer a nut that lived in the ground, about a foot down.
I was a heavenly nut that lived in the sky, way up high. Ah, such renown.

TODAY I WAS BLUE

Today I was blue because I didn't talk to you.
My heart was all a stew; I didn't know what to do.
I locked myself in my room and thought of myself as your groom.
If you don't marry me soon, there's going to be a big boom.

I searched for ways to fill my day, as every person should seek.
Happiness I knew I should find, but I find myself so very weak.
I held your picture in my hand and gently kissed the wooden frame.
In my mind, you kissed me back, for I felt it on my lips.

You see I was blue and I didn't know what to do.
I sat down in my chair and tried to take a nap, or two.
That did not work so well you know,
For when I closed my eyes I only thought of you.

I moved around all day so slow.
I wondered why the clocks had stopped.
My mind was off a minute or two.
Real concentration I could not do.

So I left my room and forced a smile,
And said to myself, "I must be in love."
"No," I said, "It can't be true.
My thinking is off. I must have the flu."

I felt of my head, but it was not hot.
The flu was gone and so was my brain.
My smile turned to a frown with a tear.
My face was lonely, like my life I fear.

Then I heard the sound of the nearby phone.
I rushed to answer. I picked it up and said, "Hello."
My hand was shaking when I heard her say,
"Hello, sweetheart. How are you today?"

She must have known I was thinking of her.
Now my whole morning was just a blur.
All of a sudden I was as alive as could be
And my heart was buzzing like the wings of a bee.

How could this be? I thought, "What the heck?"
A moment ago, I was a confused wreck.
But now my frown had turned to a smile.
Life was not sour like I'd thought for a while.

Now, the sun was shining bright in my heart.
I said to myself, "I am in love. The Spirit has spoken."
I will not refuse. Her voice was like a song.
God sent an angel to lighten my load. I was not wrong.

Today I was blue.
I didn't know what to do,

Until…

I heard her voice and all things became new.
So I said, "Hello, sweetheart. How are you?"

TWISTED HEART

I think of you both day and night.
My heart gets twisted when you are in sight.

When you reach out your hand and I take it in mine.
You smile with your eyes and make me feel fine.

When I hold you close, I feel such pleasure.
It is a gift from the Spirit, of this I am sure.

The angels smile when our love for each other shows.
They put us together, surely everyone knows.

We are so glad to share what we have as we go about.
The love in our twisted heart we won't hide, no we'll shout.

You hold my twisted heart.
And I hold yours, together or apart.

I hope it to be true for all the days we have in store.
Without your love, I would be no more.

You feel the same; I hear it in your sigh.
I will walk close by your side by and by.

Each day I rise and look at my wonder, my dear,
I give thanks to the Spirit for having you so near.

I do not deserve you, yet you're placed in my care.
I promise you, Lord, I will not despair.

Do not leave us, please guide us, Great Spirit of all.
Let our days be long and always ready when you call.

At times I think we are all alone,
Receiving special grace from his throne.

But then I think not of myself,
Realizing others sit waiting on the shelf.

They have hearts so big and pure.
They search night and day for a cure.

They long for the day they will feel a tingle.
Seeing that gentle someone among those you mingle.

She'll give him a smile and that will be their start.
At once or in time they will feel a twist of the heart.

The Spirit will say, "I give you this gift. It is my art.
I could not bear to see you two apart."

"I give this gift to all who will look.
Your name will be written in my Book."

"I am on my throne, yet I see all with eyes of love.
All good things come from above."

I trust the Spirit will send someone as you call.
If you are willing to give love your all.

Your heart will not twist if your heart is not true,
With forgiveness and gentleness flowing through.

Send love from your heart and do your best.
The Spirit will surely give you a test.

He watches from above, loving you all day and night long.
To each other he will make sure you two belong.

YOU CAN'T TAKE
AWAY MY HEART

You can't take away my heart.
My heart belongs to me.
Try as you did to make it crumble.
You only made my heart more humble.

My heart is the sunshine of my soul,
With love for all and it's never cold.
You can't take away my heart.
Although it once belonged to you.

Others could see that to you my heart was just a toy.
I knew it would never be a heart you would love with joy.
You placed it in your toy box, closed the lid, and locked the chest.
You didn't need it; I could tell, even when I tried to do my best.

For many years, my heart stayed locked in that chest, waiting for you
to open the lid. But you wanted something new; You were like a kid.
You looked around and found a new heart, but it had no love within.
You didn't even know where it had been.

It was yours for a short time and then it was gone.
And you found yourself all alone.
You opened the lid on my heart's chest and peeked in.
But then, you would close the lid again.

You gave it life and light for a short time, but it was growing old.
It could feel the winters were getting cold.
My heart became restless and broke out of the box. It was not a toy.
It had been locked up too long I thought. It knew it was time to
spread joy.

It came to life, which you did not like it strong enough to protest.
You were hoping that it had died while locked in the chest.
To your surprise, my heart was bigger, once it was in the light for all to see.
So you've been telling it lies but claiming it was the truth to me.

My heart would not listen to you anymore.
No matter how much it loved and adored.
You can't control a heart that is finally free.
No matter how long it was locked in the box unable to see.

It knew that one day it would gain enough strength to show love again
And be able to help other hearts that were trapped in pain.
You threw my heart out of the door of our home.
You left it outside along and lost to roam.

But other hearts came to my rescue, lifting and giving hope to my heart.
It found a home with good hearts, and from that place will never depart.
My heart will never be alone again; it will always love and live in the light.
But there are those who still live locked in cold chests in dark night.

When I find a chest I will open the lid, reach down with my hand, and lift out each heart.
I will tell them they're free to love and adore, for love is in them, filling each part.

YOU THOUGHT YOU HAD ME DOWN

You thought you had me down,
With your foot on my crown.
I took my hand and moved your foot.
Then I stood and wiped off the dirt and soot.

You seem bound to put me down.
You told the world that I did wrong.
You just wanted me gone the whole time.
The Spirit told me I could go, it was pastime.

The Spirit said, "You have taken your last blow.
You did your best for many years.
Now take your tears and walk away.
Go south and rest by the bay."

Day after day, I sat and listened and watched the sun glisten.
It shimmered off the water that rolled and rumbled.
Calm I became as I sat on the floor,
Listening to the waves pound the sand shore.

The beauty was there; the sound so sweet.
It kept me alive, though I was still trembling.
My eyes grew wet as I thought of the past.
But somehow I knew the dye had been cast.

Yesterday was on my mind as I wondered alone from dawn 'til dawn.
They said time will heal before you fall into a pit without a ladder.
But of course to me these words didn't matter.
Anywhere but here had to be better.

I had cared so much without care returned.
I felt my soul had been deeply burned.
Somehow I knew my life was worthwhile.
But all was quiet some time before my face could smile.

The Spirit had asked me to go,
To gain the wisdom he wanted to show.
He said, "Move forward each day though you're down and blue.
Keep trusting me to see you through."

You thought you had me down for good.
But I am free to love as I know I should.
Christ's Spirit has worked in me, a mere mortal down below.
His great love lifts me up so I can stand and take each blow.

PONDERING

ANITA

There is a girl named Anita,
Who is as pretty as a picture could be.
Maybe I care for her more than I should,
But I can't care less, that's not me.

My heart has been broken before.
And I fear it will happen again.
Maybe I've searched too hard for someone who cares.
No matter the cost, I'll bear the pain.

My life has been full of loneliness and heartbreak.
But what would life be without love's pain?
I stand by what I do each day—right or wrong.
Through it all I have seen so much gain.

I have been blessed in so many ways.
There is no way to count them all.
And because tomorrow, today will be gone.
Today I am going to have a ball.

I may be left to walk alone, belonging to no one,
If Anita refuses to be my love.
But peace will come by the spirit within my soul,
And I'll keep soaring on the wings of my dove.

ANKARA ROSE

Someone told me a few days ago that I was a great grandfather.

I thought for a while as my chest swelled with pride, and
Wondered how this could happen to a man like me?
What had I done to be so honored
By a little girl just a few days old.

I asked for some pictures and received them right away.
I printed them out and put them on display.
I stared at the photos and held (hem up to the light).
I knew in my heart that I had to hold her tight.

She lived so far away, so when would this happen?
I did not know, for I was on the mend.

I called her on the phone and we had a nice chat.
She was hard to understand; I didn't really know the language,
But I didn't let on; it wasn't the words, it was all in the tone.
She knew it was me, I could tell from her moan.

I'm almost sure she said,

"Hi, Granddad. Soon your heart will heal. Then you can come to be
with me. I will wait in my crib and do just fine as long as Mom and
Dad are near. You see I need them to bring me food once in a while
and sometimes my diaper needs changing. I am growing up fast, so
don't miss too much of the past."

I asked her, "What is your name?"

With a cute little groan and grunt she said, "Why, it's Ankara Rose."

"What a beautiful name," I told her that day,
"It won't be long before you can come out and play."

I hung up the phone and sat in my chair.
In the short time we had become a quit a pair.

As I drifted off to sleep, for it was getting late,
I rested with pride and peace was my mind.

Ankara Rose, thank you for your kind words.
They helped me so much today.
For you are my kin and I am on the mend.
Knowing that you care will help me tomorrow.

You see, my life has been long, though spotted a bit.
Don't look for the spots on any ones soul.
Look for the scares that have healed along the way.

I'll try to be a granddad that you can always love,
And hope the sun shines on both of us from above.

I am going to send you a picture of me pretty soon.
Place it on your bed and hold it tight.
For we will see each other to bolster the fight.
Yes, we both will struggle to do what is right.
Just hold out your hand and someone will catch it and pull you along.

Ankara Rose is a beautiful name.
I hope your life will be the same.

I NEVER KNEW

I never knew what it was like to have a mate and hold her heart.
I never knew what it was to think that we would never part.
This knowing would be my greatest joy.

I never knew someone who would say to me, "You are more my life than I."
I never knew how it felt to be held by her and know that it was true.
There is a force out there called love, and many know it is a wonder.

Yet...

I have known what it is like to love someone and hold her heart.
I have known what it is to see the stars in her eyes coming from the glow in my own.

I've known someone I would die for in a flash.
But now...that is all in the past.

I sent my heart in her direction, hoping she would place it next to hers.
But it was as if she said, "I don't need your heart. I have one of my own."

The years went by...

I lived with hope that someday, someday...she would accept my heart.
I lived in this hope for three decades, until I knew it was time to part.
I picked my heart up that day and walked away.

I finally knew she had no love for me, and yet, it was no real surprise.
I always knew it, I think. Yes, I knew it all along.

Some will ask, "Why did you stay so long?"
Others will say, "You are running away!"

If you have lived your life with no one to hold your heart,
If you have led a lonely life, then you know what it is to hold out
your hand,
Stretched out as far as you can, but find no one did there to ease your
pain.

Don't feel sorry for me. You see, I still have my heart.
And hope I will, though it may be in vain.
No matter what they say, I have experienced much gain.

You must love with all your heart, not holding back.
Don't hold back, looking for someone better.

If…

You never knew what it was like to have a mate and hold her heart,
Pick up your heart and walk away.
The sun will shine on you some day.
And you will hear someone say, "You are more my life than I."

I SERVED TOO

I served too, as Daddy did.
I didn't have a pack and a mess hall kit.
I didn't have a uniform for all to see
That I loved my country, the same as he.

When Daddy left and went to war.
All we had was a beat-up old car.
Momma cried and cried as Daddy left us that day.
We didn't have a big house that sat by the bay.

We only had a tenant house that sat in a field.
We didn't have a bank account, and
The coffee can was down to a jingle.
I knew that year, there would be no Kris Kringle.

I was only eleven when Daddy marched off to serve.
There was no way faith was going to throw us a curve.
Mama looked at me and said, "Son, we are going to have to work and
save every dime."
I hoped someday it would come our time.

They put me in the fields with grown-ups all around.
They didn't pay me much attention, but I held my ground.
All day and half the night, Mama and I worked to pay our way.
I even heard them say, "He works hard. The kids okay."

Food was scarce and hunger I felt.
I would go to the woods to track down some guineas.
I'd steal their eggs when I could find their nest.
Then bring them home to be scrambled at best.

My sister helped Mama with cooking and care.
We did have shoes; our feet were not bare.
One day Daddy came home and he said he could stay.
Now we were no longer alone day after day.

Daddy built us a home that we could call our own.
I realized that while Daddy was gone I had grown.
I'd learned how to plow and I learned how to hoe.
But most of all I learned how to care for what we had and the love
we shared.

As I stand up and salute our Veterans, I shed a tear.
Proud I am of all of them.
I think of all those that served at home through sweat and tears.
Proud I am of all of them.
I remember how as a boy, I served too.
Proud I am.
I served too.

I WILL ALWAYS WONDER

I will always wonder why I fell for you.
Maybe it was because you were young and beautiful.
Maybe it was because I was looking for someone like you.
Maybe it was because your eyes met mine.
Yes, I will always wonder.

But this I know…

I lost my heart on that Spring day.
And I am so glad in so many ways.
I would not have wanted it any other way.
My heart needed something and I thought you were it.

For many years I have believed,
You thought of me as I thought of you.
Two people together,
Who were meant to be.

I wasn't very smart, and not well trained,
But I was willing to learn and work hard for us.
I had big dreams and planned for the best.
For you and the girls, that was my task.

I had the world on a string,
And no one could contest the love that we shared.
I think of those times with glee in my heart.
From me, no one can ever take that part.

Nothing can last forever, I guess.
That doesn't mean I didn't want it to.
I was surely blessed by you and the girls.

But the string broke and the world drifted away.
I tried to hold on for as long as I could.
I grew tired and weary and I guess you could say,
I was lost and alone with no one to love me.

It's a lonely feeling when love goes one way.
I felt second hand and unable to please the love of my life.
And I knew you didn't care if I came home at night.

So what was I to do? I had failed as a husband.
I kept moving forward the best that I could,
With hope in my heart that love would return but to no avail.
I spent my years thinking I could not fail.

It takes two loves to make a home.
But you can live if there is only one.

BAD

I have been bad to someone today.
I got the best of them you see.
Clever was I to poke him in the eye.
And then, I watched him cry.

I heard my mother say, "You have been bad."
She was mad and sent me away.
I went outside with a silly grin.
I went next door to play with a friend.

I was feeling good about being bad.
It made me feel tough and strong.
So I thought I'd poke my friend in the eye,
And then watch him cry.

So I poked my friend in the eye, but he did not cry.
He looked at me and said, "Why did you do that?"
I gave him a grin,
Until his fist hit my chin.

He looked down at me and said,
"I didn't hit you because I want to be bad.
I hit you because I don't want you to be bad.
I wanted you to be my friend, not try to make me sad."

I didn't know what to say to my friend,
And wondered why I poked him in the eye.
He gave me his hand and pulled me off the ground.
He said, "Now go away, maybe I'll see you around."

I thought for a while as I warmed the front step.
I have no friend, not even my Mom.
Maybe being bad is not for me, I thought with a sigh.
All alone I sat, as a tear dropped from my eye.

I realized I did not like being bad.
And decided to leave bad behind for good.
My brother walked out with a big old ball.
"What would you like to play? It is your call."

Form that moment on, I knew good was good,
And bad is bad and not for me.
I don't want to be all alone in the end.
I want to be a good friend.

Bad…it's not for you!

MORNING TIME

I woke up this morning at the crack of dawn.
I asked my Lord, "Why am I alone?"
He said, "Don't worry, my son, it won't be for long."

I know he is not angry, for he has given me his grace.
My sins have been forgiven, and I live with his Spirit.
I became calm as I thought of his presence,

And I leapt out of bed as a smile crossed my face.
"Sorry, my Lord, for that bit of doubt.
I know you have a lot of clout."

It was my morning, and it was meant to be shared.
So I dialed her number just to hear her voice.
All I heard was an answering machine.

But all was not lost; I did hear her voice.
She said, "Leave a message, if you please."
Now I know she's not a tease, so she meant every word.

I said, "It's just me. Call me when you have time."

I know an angel voice when I hear it.
I asked the Lord, "Are you going to make her mine?"
All he said was, "Patience, my son. You must give it time."

He explained, "Earth angels are very few, so we must be careful.
It will be my choice. Just love her and treat her with kindness.
And someday I might ask her to give you her heart."

But I wondered if she might need me now, and asked my Lord,
"How will I know when this happens?"
He said, "Son, are you having a bit of doubt?
Don't you know I have a lot of clout?"

MY HOSPITAL ROOM

Today is the day I will leave this room.
A one-room palace I used for a week.
The floors do not creak.
The walls do not talk.
But when I push a button, the room comes to life.

There are no spirits left here to roam.
They've all gone home where they do not moan.
But they will always remember this one-room palace.

Each morning when I wake, I am in my bedroom.
But soon I move to the morning room,
Where I have my coffee and eat a bit.
Then on to the bathroom where I shave and refresh.
Next it's the sitting room, where I sit in my easy chair.
Here I can see the sun as it shines outside my palace.
I rest in my chair until it is dark again,
Then back to the bedroom for a night of rest.

Each morning as I sit in my easy chair,
I wait for my daughters to appear at my door.
Don't tell them you know, but I needed them so.
If there are spots on this paper, it's a drip from my nose.
For why should I cry?
I live in a palace.

Someone came by and asked if I needed anything.
I said, "No, I just have heart pains."
They smiled and responded, "I'll be back later.
But if you need me, just push the button."

Here my palace has everything I need.
They bring me my food and make up my bed.
They shower me with attention all day and night.
Whatever will I do, when I leave this palace?

I closed my eyes and silent I felt as
I heard all the prayers that were sent to me.
I opened my heart and received them all in,
Then opened my eyes to see the doctor grin.
"Well, we are sending you home," he said as he left.
"Your time in the palace has come to an end."

So I put on my clothes and packed my bag.
And waited for the rolling chair to wheel me outside.

I wondered who would live in this palace next.
I hoped their stay would be as pleasant as mine.
I will leave a little of me behind.
Maybe it will help the next person who comes here to stay.
For who is to say what could happen in this palace.

My palace you see is only one room,
And they had me hooked up, so I could not leave.
But now I am free.
I am a new born.

There is another drop on this paper I see.
I'll have to do something about that nose of mine.
Why should I cry?
I lived in a palace.

THE BEGGAR MAN

As I look left and as I look right,
I see so many with their hand held out.
"Give to me for I am poor."
"Give to me for I am hungry."
There is no doubt that they do need,
But I wonder why they are asking me.
What I have, I want to keep.

So I walk on by with my head held high.
I work so hard for the things I have.
Why don't they work and they could be like me.
I went on to my office on the very top floor.
I looked out my window at the beggar man below.
I closed my eyes and thought, "Please, go away."
Then the sun came through the glass.

It was so bright I could not see.
I looked up toward the light and watched a cloud obscure the bright.
I said, "Thank you cloud for helping me."
"Without your help, I was blind."
I looked back down to the beggar man.
To my surprise he was lying on the ground.
I rushed back down to find him there.

He said, "I'm all right.
The sun blinded me and I lost my way.
I tripped and fell and could not get up.
So I asked God to give me a hand.
My prayer was answered, for you are here.
Give me your hand, so I may stand,
And be like you and any other man.

I once had an office like you.
Such fine clothes I always wore.
Every day you pass me, I pray for you,
To never be poor and hungry like me.
I once had an office, over there,
Until life gave me more than I could bare.
Now it's hard to find anyone to care.

You see, Sir, the money that I get here on this corner,
I share with those who really need it.
All I need are rags to wear and a little food to keep me here."
Then he looked at me and walked away.
He turned and smiled, his face was aglow.
As I looked at his face, I was looking at me.
I fell on my knees and tears filled my eyes.

I think I was talking to God Himself.

WOMAN (GOD'S GIFT)

God gives us many gifts, you know.
To us…humans…here below.
As I rise each day, I have so many.
I know the gifts are plenty.
They fill my heart with thoughts of good.
They make my face smile, as it should.

I opened my door and walked out into the hall,
Looking for someone to share my smile.
I was off to the break room where I knew I would find a friend.
For there was no one in this home that I would offend.

The sound of laughter spilled out of the room.
There was even someone trying to croon.
I stopped and listened to God's gift of laughter for all.
It sounded so good to me out here in the hall.

So I walked into the room with a smile on my face.
I knew I was surely in the right place.
"Good morning to you," I said with a shout.
With smiles they all turned about.

"And good morning to you," they said in return.
I shook hands with the men and hugged the women.
I realized then, God's beautiful gift of touch,
Was so powerful and one we all need so much.

The gifts from God each day, I share.
They free my spirit with loving care.
So when adversity comes my way,
I ask my God to help me not sway.

The gifts he gives are greater by far,
Than the pain he sends to teach us are.
My heart is comforted by all God's gift to date.
But the greatest gift for the human race is a mate.

They call her woman; God's greatest gift I think.
Some have tried to bring her to the brink.
She stands alone, so much of the time.
Woman suffers unjustly, accused of no crime.

But woman will stand with you or alone.
She will be there even when you are gone.
The strength she shows is tender and dear,
And is greater than the strongest tree that is near.

Take pride O woman for who you are
You are greater by far.
I need your beauty and your charm.
They are a reason to be born.

O man if you do not feel this way,
Cleanse your heart and change today.
For woman's love can one's spirits lift.
Oh yes, woman is his greatest gift.

ABOUT THE AUTHOR

William was born on a sharecroppers farm in North Carolina in a house that was full of love and worked for the same firm for 35 years. Married, two daughters, three grandchildren, and two great-grandchildren.

I believe Jesus Christ wrote these inspirations that are in this book; he just wrote them for him.

CPSIA information can be obtained
at www.ICGtesting.com
Printed in the USA
BVHW031105220719
554056BV00011B/411/P